ristmas 2006

To Alice

Best wishes

Maresa .

Treasury of
Prayers

COMPILED
BY
DEBORAH CASSIDI

continuum
LONDON • NEW YORK

Continuum
The Tower Building
11 York Road, London SE1 7NX
370 Lexington Avenue, New York, NY 10017-6503

**This book contains extracts from Favourite Prayers – chosen by people
from all walks of life, compiled by Deborah Cassidi, Continuum, 1998**

British Library Cataloguing-in-Publication Data
A catalogue record for this book is available from the British Library.

ISBN 0 8264 6702 4

Edited, designed and produced by
Delian Bower and Vic Giolitto

Printed in Hong Kong

The Lord's Prayer

Our Father, who art in heaven, hallowed be thy name;
thy kingdom come; thy will be done,
on earth as it is in heaven.
Give us this day our daily bread.
And forgive us our trespasses,
as we forgive those who trespass against us.
And lead us not into temptation; but deliver us from evil.
For thine is the kingdom, the power, and the glory,
for ever and ever.
Amen.

SANDRINGHAM, NORFOLK

O Lord, the creator of the universe and author of the laws of nature, inspire in us thy servants the will to ensure the survival of all the species of animals and plants, which you have given to share this planet with us. Help us to understand that we have a responsibility for them and that 'having dominion' does not mean that you have given us the right to exploit the living world without thought for the consequences. Through him who taught us that Solomon in all his glory could not compare with the beauty of the flowers in the field.

HRH The Duke of Edinburgh

Courage

SIR ANTONY ACLAND, *former Provost of Eton College*

Grant us, O Lord, the Royalty of inward happiness and the serenity that comes from living close to Thee. Daily renew in us the sense of joy, and let Thy eternal spirit dwell in our souls and bodies, filling every corner of our hearts with light and gladness. So that, bearing about with us the infection of a good courage, we may be diffusers of life, and meet all that comes, of good or ill, even death itself, with gallant and high-hearted happiness; giving Thee thanks always for all things.

Robert Louis Stevenson (1850–94)

'A prayer for those brave people who remain cheerful under adversity when courage is indeed infectious.'

THE REVD RUPERT BLISS,
retired naval officer, teacher and mathematician

A Breton Fisherman's Prayer

Dear God, be good to me,
The sea is so large and our boat is so small.

Anon.

COLONEL JOHN BLASHFORD-SNELL, *explorer and scientist*

O Lord God, when Thou givest to Thy servants to endeavour any great matter, grant us to know that it is not the beginning, but the continuing of the same unto the end, until it be thoroughly finished, which yieldeth the true glory: through Him who for the finishing of Thy work laid down His life, our Redeemer Jesus Christ. Amen.

Sir Francis Drake (c. 1540–96)

'I chose this because it was very much on my mind when launching Operation Drake in 1978 and Operation Raleigh. It is said that there are no atheists before battle. Imagining how Drake felt, I hoped it would help us also to succeed. Indeed it did!'

JOHN CALLEAR, *veterinary surgeon*

I bring this prayer to you, Lord,
For you alone can give
What one cannot demand but from oneself.
Give me, Lord, what you have left over,
Give me what no one ever asks you for.
I don't ask for rest or quiet,
whether of soul or of body;
I don't ask for wealth.
Nor for success, not even for health perhaps,
That sort of thing you get asked for so much
That you can't have any of it left.
I want insecurity, anxiety,
I want storm and strife
and I want you to give me these once and for all
since I shan't have the courage to ask you for them.
Give me, Lord, what you have left over,
Give me what the others want nothing to do with.
But give me courage too
And strength and faith.
For you alone can give
What one cannot demand but from oneself.

Written in the Western Desert by André Zirnheld, a Free French member of the SAS and a friend of David Stirling, its leader. Translated by Professor Alan Steele, Edinburgh University.

MARY CROSSLEY, *carpet manufacturer, Halifax*

O God, early in the morning I cry to you. Help me to pray and to concentrate my thoughts on you: I cannot do this alone.

In me there is darkness. But with you there is light; I am lonely, but you do not leave me; I am feeble in heart, but with you there is help; I am restless, but with you there is peace. In me there is bitterness, but with you there is patience; I do not understand your ways, but you know the way for me.

Restore me to liberty, and enable me so to live now that I may answer before you and before men. Lord, whatever this day may bring, your name be praised. Amen.

Dietrich Bonhoeffer, (1906–45)
Written in prison while he was awaiting execution.

PETER AND PENNY ELLIS, *retired barrister and wife*

The Rune of Saint Patrick

At Tara today in this fateful hour
I place all Heaven with its power
and the sun with its brightness,
and the snow with its whiteness,
and fire with all the strength it hath,
and lightning with its rapid wrath,
and the winds with their swiftness along their path,

and the sea with its deepness,
and the rocks with their steepness,
and the earth with its starkness:
   all these I place,
    by God's almighty help and grace
between myself and the powers of darkness.

James Clarence Mangan (1803–49)

JAMES GALWAY, *flautist*

In the Morning

O God, our Father, deliver us this day from all that would keep us from serving Thee and from serving our fellowmen as we ought.

Deliver us from all coldness of heart; and grant that neither our hand nor our heart may ever remain shut to the appeal of someone's need.

Deliver us from all weakness of will; from the indecision which cannot make up its mind; from the irresolution which cannot abide by a decision once it is made; from the inability to say No to the tempting voices which come to us from inside and from outside.

Deliver us from all failure in endeavour; from being too easily discouraged; from giving up and giving in too soon; from allowing any task to defeat us, because it is difficult.

Grant unto us this day the love which is generous in help; the determination which is steadfast in decision; the perseverance which is enduring unto the end; through Jesus Christ our Lord.

William Barclay

RICHARD ORMOND,
former Director of the National Maritime Museum, Greenwich

A Vailima Prayer

Give us grace and strength
to forbear and to persevere.
Give us courage and gaiety
and the quiet mind.
Spare to us our friends, soften
to us our enemies. Bless us
if it may be in all our
innocent endeavours. If it
may not, give us the strength
to encounter that which is to
come, that we may be brave
in peril, constant in tribulation,
temperate in wrath.
And in all changes of fortune
And down to the gates of death
Loyal and loving
To one another.

Robert Louis Stevenson (1850–94)

Death

TIMOTHY AND ELIZABETH CAPON,
company director and art gallery guide

Keep me in Thy love
As Thou wouldst that all should be kept in mine.
May everything in this my being be directed to Thy glory
And may I never despair
For I am under Thy hand
And in Thee is all power and goodness.

Dag Hammarskjöld (1905–61)

Those who die in Grace go no further than God,
and God is very near.

BRIAN CARPENTER, *postman*

The Lord is my shepherd; I shall not want.
He maketh me to lie down in green pastures: he leadeth
me beside the still waters.
He restoreth my soul: he leadeth me in the paths of right-
eousness
for his name's sake.

Psalm 23, verses 1–3 (Authorized Version)

NEIL DURDEN-SMITH, *company director, Lord's Taverner*

The Ship

What is dying?
I am standing on the sea shore,
a ship sails in the morning breeze
and starts for the ocean.
She is an object of beauty
and I stand watching her
till at last she fades
on the horizon
and someone at my side says:
'She is gone.'
Gone! Where?
Gone from my sight – that is all.
She is just as large in the masts, hull and spars
as she was when I saw her,
and just as able to bear her load of living
freight to its destination.
The diminished size and total loss of sight is in me,
not in her,
and just at the moment when someone at my side says,
'She is gone'
there are others who are watching her coming,
and other voices take up a glad shout:
'There she comes!'
 – and that is dying.

Bishop Brent (1862–1926)

PAUL HEIM, *barrister*

Let Man Remember

Let man remember all the days of his life
He moves at the grave's request.
He goes a little journey every day
And thinks he is at rest;
Like someone lying on board a ship
Which flies at the wind's behest

Moses ibn Ezra (c.1055–c.1137)

Moses ibn Ezra, a philosopher, Biblical commentator, poet and astronomer, was probably a native of Granada. He survived both the persecution of the Jews in 1066 and the destruction of the city by Berbers in 1090. He travelled widely in Europe, including London. This version was translated by David Goldstein (1933–81), rabbi and curator of Hebrew Books and Manuscripts at the British Library.

SIR ANTONY JAY, *scriptwriter and author*

Easter Hymn

If in that Syrian garden, ages slain,
You sleep, and know not you are dead in vain,
Nor even in dreams behold how dark and bright
Ascends in smoke and fire by day and night
The hate you died to quench and could but fan,
Sleep well and see no morning, son of man.
But if, the grave rent and the stone rolled by,
At the right hand of majesty on high
You sit, and sitting so remember yet
Your tears, your agony and bloody sweat,
Your cross and passion and the life you gave,
Bow hither out of heaven and see and save.

A. E. Housman (1859–1936)

SIR ROBIN KNOX-JOHNSTON, *master mariner*

O Lord, if we are to die, I would rather it were in pro-
ceeding than in retreating.

'Attributed to John Davis (1550–1605), probably the greatest
Elizabethan navigator.'

NIGEL HOPKINS, *refuse lorry driver*

Abide with me; fast falls the eventide;
The darkness deepens; Lord, with me abide;
When other helpers fail, and comforts flee,
Help of the helpless, O abide with me.

Henry F. Lyte (1793–1847)

THE REVD DR SUSAN RAMSARAN, *parish priest*

O Lord, may the end of my life be the best of it;
may my closing acts be my best acts;
and may the best of my days be the day when I shall
   meet Thee.

Unknown source

JOHN TYDEMAN, *retired Head of Drama, BBC Radio 4*

Bring us, O Lord God, at our last awakening into the house and gate of heaven; to enter into that gate and dwell in that house, where there shall be no darkness nor dazzling, but one equal light; no noise nor silence, but one equal music; no fears nor hopes, but one equal possession; no ends, nor beginnings, but one equal eternity; in the habitations of thy glory and dominion, world without end. Amen.

John Donne (1572–1631)

PAT STUART, *diplomat's wife and housewife*

We seem to give them back to You, O God, who gave them to us. Yet as You did not lose them in giving, so we do not lose them by their return. Not as the world gives, do You give, O lover of souls. What You give, take not away, for what is Yours is ours also if we are Yours. And life is eternal and love is immortal, and death is only a horizon, and a horizon is nothing save the limit of our sight. Lift us up, strong Son of God, that we may see further; cleanse our eyes that we may see more clearly; draw us closer to Yourself that we may know ourselves to be nearer to our loved ones who are with You. And while You prepare a place for us, prepare us also for that happy place that where You are we may be also for evermore.

Bishop Brent (1862–1926)

Faith

PETER ALLISS, *professional golfer and TV commentator*

Fear knocked at the door. Faith opened it and there was no one there.

'This is the family saying at times of adversity but the source is unknown.'

ELIZABETH ALLSOP, *farm smallholder (mixed stock)*

Newness of Life

O most merciful Father, for Thy most innocent Son's sake: and since He has spread His arms upon the cross, to receive the whole world, O Lord, shut out none of us (who are now fallen before the throne of Thy majesty and Thy mercy) from the benefit of His merits; but with as many of us as begin their conversion and newness of life this minute, this minute, O God, begin Thou Thy account with them and put all that is past out of Thy remembrance. Accept our humble thanks for all Thy mercies; and continue and enlarge them upon the whole church.

John Donne (1572–1631)

PRISCILLA BARKER, *housewife*

Give us, O God, the vision which can see Thy love in the world in spite of human failure. Give us the faith to trust Thy goodness in spite of our ignorance and weakness. Give us the knowledge that we continue to pray with understanding hearts, and to do what each one of us can do to set forward the coming of the day of universal peace. Amen.

A prayer offered in space on Christmas Eve, 1968,
by Apollo VIII's commander, Frank Borman

His Eminence Cardinal Cahal Daly,
former Archbishop of Armagh

Prayer of Abandonment

Father,
I abandon myself into your hands;
do with me what you will.
Whatever you may do I thank you:
I am ready for all, I accept all.
Let only your will be done in me,
and in all your creatures.
I wish nothing more than this, O Lord.
Into your hands I commend my soul:
I offer it to you
with all the love of my heart,
for I do love you, Lord,
and so I need to give myself,
to surrender myself into your hands,
without reserve,
and with boundless confidence,
because you are my Father.

Charles de Foucauld (1858–1916),
translated by Cardinal Daly

Charles de Foucauld initially led a dissipated life but after his military service (distinguished by its bravery) in the Sahara, this changed. He became a Trappist hermit in the Sahara, respected by and serving the Tuareg and other Muslim desert tribes. Tragically, he was murdered by a member of a fanatical sect. Soon beatified, his life inspired the founding of both the Little Brothers and Little Sisters of Jesus.

BRIAN IRVINE, *football player (Aberdeen F.C.)*

Because He Lives

God sent His Son, they called Him Jesus;
He came to love, heal and forgive;
He lived and died to buy my pardon,
an empty grave is there to prove my Saviour lives.
Because He lives I can face tomorrow;
because He lives all fear is gone;
because I know He holds the future,
and life is worth the living
just because He lives.

William J. Gaither (copyright © 1971 Kingsway's Thankyou Music)

CAPTAIN RICHARD MERYON, *RN*

For this cause I bow my knees unto the Father of our
  Lord Jesus Christ,
That Christ may dwell in your hearts by faith; that ye,
  being rooted and grounded in love,
May be able to comprehend with all the saints what is
  the breadth, and length, and depth, and height;
And to know the love of Christ, which passeth knowledge, that ye might be filled with all the
fulness of God.

Ephesians 3, verses 14 and 17–19 (Authorized Version)

LADY MORSE, *London tourist guide*

[And] I said to the man who stood at the gate of the year: 'Give me a light that I may tread safely into the unknown.' And he replied: 'Go out into the darkness and put your hand into the hand of God. That shall be better than a light and safer than a known way.'

Minnie Louise Haskins, teacher and writer

CHARLOTTE MORETON, *ecologist*

Be sober, be vigilant; because your adversary the devil, as a roaring lion, walketh about, seeking whom he may devour:
Whom resist steadfast in the faith.

1 Peter 5, verses 8–9 (Authorized Version)

THE WESTMINSTER ABBEY CHORISTERS

O Lord our God, give us by your Holy Spirit a willing heart and a ready hand to use all your gifts to your praise and glory; through Jesus Christ our Lord.

Thomas Cranmer (1489–1556)

I believe in the sun even when it is not shining.
I believe in love even when I cannot feel it.
I believe in God, even when he is silent.

*Words found written on the cell wall of a
Jewish prisoner in Cologne*

O Jesus, Son of God, who was silent before Pilate, do not let us wag our tongues without thinking of what we are to say and how to say it.

Irish Gaelic prayer

FORGIVENESS

CAROL AUGER, *Lambeth street market stall-holder*

Dear Lord and Father of mankind,
Forgive our foolish ways!
Re-clothe us in our rightful mind,
In purer lives thy service find.
In deeper reverence praise.

J. G. Whittier (1807–92)

KEITH, *life-sentenced prisoner*

Dear God,
I hold up all my weakness to your strength,
My failure to your faithfulness,
My sinfulness to your perfection,
My loneliness to your compassion,
My small pain to your agony on the cross.
Amen.

Keith wrote the prayer from which this is taken as an adaptation
of one he found inscribed on the wall of his prison cell.

LADY BUTLER OF SAFFRON WALDEN

God be in my head, and in my understanding;
God be in my eyes, and in my looking;
God be in my mouth, and in my speaking;
God be in my heart, and in my thinking;
God be at my end, and at my departing.

Sarum Primer (1558)

THE RT. HON. LADY JUSTICE BUTLER-SLOSS,
Lady Justice of Appeal

Shew me thy ways, O Lord; teach me thy paths.
Lead me in thy truth, and teach me: for thou art the God
of my salvation; on thee do I wait all the day.
Remember, O Lord, thy tender mercies and thy loving-
kindnesses; for they have been ever of old.
Remember not the sins of my youth, nor my
transgressions: according to thy mercy; remember thou
me for thy goodness' sake, O Lord.

Psalm 25, verses 4–7 (Authorized Version)

JOE PARHAM, *solicitor's clerk*

Love

Love bade me welcome: yet my soul drew back,
                Guiltie of dust and sin.
But quick-ey'd Love, observing me grow slack
                From my first entrance in,
Drew nearer to me, sweetly questioning,
                If I lack'd anything.
A guest, I answer'd, worthy to be here:
                Love said, you shall be he.
I the unkinde, ungrateful? Ah my deare,
                I cannot look on thee.
Love took my hand and smiling did reply:
                Who made the eyes but I?
Truth, Lord, but I have marr'd them: let my shame
                Go where it doth deserve.
And know you not, sayes Love, who bore the blame?
                My deare, then I will serve.
You must sit down, sayes Love, and taste my meat:
                So I did sit and eat.

George Herbert (1593–1633)

THE RT. HON. THE LADY WARNOCK,
*House of Lords cross-bencher, philosopher, Chairman of the
Committee of Inquiry on Human Fertilisation*

Lord Jesus, think on me,
Nor let me go astray;
Through darkness and perplexity
Point Thou the heavenly way.

Lord Jesus, think on me,
When flows the tempest high:
When on doth rush the enemy
O Saviour, be Thou nigh.

*Bishop Synesius of Cyrene (Bishop of Ptolemais) (375–430);
translated by Allen W. Chatfield (1808–96)*

HAROLD WRIGHT, *retired thatcher*

Rock of ages, cleft for me,
Let me hide myself in thee;
Let the water and the blood,
From thy riven side which flowed,
Be of sin the double cure:
Cleanse me from its guilt and power.

Augustus M. Toplady (1740–78)

I cannot teach you how to pray in words. God listens not to your words save when He himself utters them through your lips. And I cannot teach you the prayer of the seas and the forests and the mountains. But you who are born of the mountains and the forests and the seas can find their prayer in your heart.

From The Prophet *by Kahlil Gibran (1883–1931)*

God's Presence

DEBORAH CASSIDI, *retired doctor*

Jesus, tender Shepherd, hear me,
Bless thy little lamb tonight,
Through the darkness be thou near me,
Keep me safe till morning light.

Through this day thy hand has led me,
And I thank thee for thy care.
Thou hast clothed me, warmed and fed me,
Listen to my evening prayer.

Let my sins be all forgiven,
Bless the friends I love so well;
Take me, when I die, to heaven,
Happy there with thee to dwell.

Mary D. Duncan (1814–40)

'As a child I said this prayer nightly with my mother or grand-mother. It has been used thus for four generations of the family.'

DR SHEILA CASSIDY,
ex-prisoner of conscience, cancer physician and psychotherapist

A Prayer for All God's Children

Lord of all hopefulness, Lord of all Joy – we pray for those who have lost hope and courage this day. We pray for the sick: especially those struggling with terminal cancer, AIDS or motor neurone disease. We pray too for prisoners, for refugees, hostages and all who are trapped in unhappy relationships or problems of addiction. We think, too, of the mentally ill: the schizophrenics, the depressed, and those whose personality is crippled by violence, neglect or abuse. We pray especially for those tempted to kill themselves this day, and for those so twisted that they would kill another. More than anything, O Lord, we pray for the children: for the street-children of the developing world, all orphans and refugees, for the hungry, for all who sleep rough on our own streets, and those who are unloved or abused. Open your heart, O Loving God, and fill it with these your children.

Written by Sheila Cassidy

JOHN CONTEH,
World Light Heavyweight Boxing Champion 1974

If you live in the shelter of Elyon and make your
home in the shadow of Shaddai,
you can say to Yahweh, 'My refuge and my fortress,
my God in whom I trust!'

Psalm 91, verses 1 and 2 (The Jerusalem Translation of the Bible,
used by many, including Catholic and Protestant denominations and
the Jehovah's Witnesses)

DAME JUDI DENCH, *actress*

O Lord! Thou knowest how busy I must be this day: If I
forget Thee do not thou forget me.

Prayer of Sir Jacob Astley (1579–1652) before the battle of Edgehill
on 13 October 1642, found in Sir Philip Warwick's memoirs, 1701

FIONA FRASER,
leader of an inter-faith group

O Father, give the spirit power to climb
to the fountain of all light, and be purified.
Break through the mists of earth, the weight
of the clod,
Shine forth in splendour, Thou that art calm weather,
And quiet resting place for the faithful souls.
To see Thee is the end and the beginning,
Thou carriest us, and Thou dost go before,
Thou art the journey, and the journey's end.

Boethius (c.480–c.524)

Pain That Heals

Let the healing grace of your love, O Lord, so transform
me that I may play my part in the transfiguration of the
world from a place of suffering, death and corruption to
a realm of infinite light, joy and love. Make me so obe-
dient to your spirit that my life may become a place of
living prayer, and a witness to your unfailing presence.

Martin Israel

SHEELAH HORSFIELD, *gardener*

Celtic Blessing from the Iona Community

Deep peace of the running wave to you,
deep peace of the flowing air to you,
deep peace of the quiet earth to you,
deep peace of the shining stars to you,
deep peace of the Son of peace to you.

Source unknown (early Scottish)

Come Holy Dove

When I feel alone Your Presence is
ever with me.
Come Holy Dove, cover with love.
When I feel weak your strength will seek me.
Come Holy Dove, cover with love.
Spirit be about my head,
Spirit peace around me shed,
Spirit light about my way,
Spirit guardian night and day.
Come Holy Dove,
Cover with love.

David Adam

MARY IRWIN,
*widow of Col. John Irwin, of Apollo XV, whose 'moon walks' in the
Hadley-Apennines area of the Moon totalled over 18 hours*

High Flight

Oh! I have slipped the surly bonds of earth
And danced the skies on laughter-silvered wings;
Sunward I've climbed, and joined the tumbling mirth
Of sun-split clouds … and done a hundred things
You have not dreamed of … wheeled and soared and swung
High in the sunlit silence. Hov'ring there
I've chased the shouting wind along, and flung
My eager craft through footless hall of air.

Up, up the long, delirious, burning blue
I've topped the wind-swept heights with easy grace
Where never lark, nor even eagle flew …
And, while with silent lifting mind I've trod
The high untrespassed sanctity of space,
Put out my hand and touched the face of God.

John Gillespie Magee, Jr (1922–41)

TIM NEWELL, *prison governer*

Keep me as the apple of an eye: hide me under the
shadow of thy wings.

Psalm 17, verse 8 (Book of Common Prayer)

'I use this verse at times of difficulty or when things are going well.
It has been a source of strength for many years and puts me in the
knowledge of God's all-present love.'

SIR HARRY SECOMBE, *singer and entertainer*

O Lord, support us all the day long of this troublous life,
until the shades lengthen and the evening comes, the
busy world is hushed, the fever of life is over, and our
work done.

Then, Lord, in Thy mercy, grant us safe lodging, a holy
rest, and peace at the last, through Jesus Christ, our
Lord. Amen.

John Henry Newman (1801–90)

PHILIP STURROCK, *publisher*

Christ in Woolworth's

I did not think to find you there –
Crucifixes, large and small,
Sixpence and threepence, on a tray,
Among the artificial pearls
Paste rings, tin watches, beads of glass.

It seemed so strange to find you there
Fingered by people coarse and crass,
Who had no reverence at all.
Yet – what is it you would say?
'For these I hang upon my cross,
For these the agony and loss,
Though heedlessly they pass Me by.'
Dear Lord forgive such fools as I
Who thought it strange to find you there
When you are with us everywhere.

Teresa Hooley

The Rt. Revd Abbot Timothy Wright,
Abbot of Ampleforth

When God Made You

When
God
made
you
there
was
silence
in
heaven
for
five
minutes.
Then
God
said:
'How come I never thought of that before?'

From Perhaps God *(1985) by Ralph Wright OSB*

'This prayer by my brother attracts me because it highlights the truth that only God can understand the uniqueness which is each one of us.'

Love

BARONESS JAMES OF HOLLAND PARK (P. D. JAMES),
author

O Lord, who hast taught us that all our doings without charity are nothing worth; Send thy Holy Ghost, and pour into our hearts that most excellent gift of charity, the very bond of peace and of all virtues, without which whosoever liveth is counted dead before thee: Grant this for thine only Son Jesus Christ's sake. Amen.

Collect for the Sunday called Quinquagesima, Book of Common Prayer

'When I was at school in Ludlow, we were taught the Collect for each Sunday, so that these prayers, so pregnant with meaning, entered my consciousness early, becoming part of my religious and literary heritage. This Collect, which has a medieval origin, is a favourite of mine and one of Cranmer's most beautiful prayers.'

SIR CLIFF RICHARD, *singer*

When I survey the wondrous cross
On which the Prince of Glory died,
My richest gain I count but loss,
And pour contempt on all my pride.

Were the whole realm of nature mine,
That were an offering far too small;
Love so amazing, so divine,
Demands my soul, my life, my all.

Isaac Watts (1674–1748)

BRIDGET MORETON, *artist*

Enlighten my soul that she may find her life and joy in
Thee, until, transported out of herself by the excess of
her happiness, she binds herself to Thee.

Dag Hammarskjöld (1905–61), translated by W. H. Auden

ROSEMARY VEREY, *gardener and author*

O God, who hast prepared for them that love thee such good things as pass man's understanding; Pour into our hearts such love toward thee, that we, loving thee above all things, may obtain thy promises, which exceed all that we can desire; through Jesus Christ our Lord. Amen.

Collect for the sixth Sunday after Trinity, Book of Common Prayer

ELIZABETH WALROND,
Sunday School teacher, mother and farmer's wife

Lord Jesus, take me this day and use me.
Take my lips and speak through them.
Take my mind and think through it.
Take my will and act through it,
and fill my heart with love for you.

From Unto the Hills

MAJOR-GENERAL CHARLES VYVYAN, *former Head of the British Defence Staff, Washington*

Prayer for a Loved One

Thou who knowest so much and lovest so many, bless, I pray Thee, my dearest love; comfort her and be with her, guide her and be near her; and let Thy light so shine upon her that she may see it and follow it and come at last unto Thy everlasting Kingdom. Amen.

Charles Vyvyan

Command what Thou wilt, but give what Thou commandest; above all things give me the strength to be Thy child on earth as Thou art my Father in Heaven; that in all that I think and say and do I may reflect Thy love, Thy life and Thy understanding. Amen.

Charles Vyvyan

J. P. R. WILLIAMS, *Welsh Rugby Union*
international player 1969–1981, consultant orthopaedic surgeon

Love divine, all loves excelling,
Joy of Heaven, to earth come down,
Fix in us Thy humble dwelling,
All Thy faithful mercies crown;
Jesu, Thou art all compassion,
Pure unbounded love Thou art;
Visit us with Thy salvation,
Enter every trembling heart.

Charles Wesley (1707–88)

Nature

JOHN COLDEBANK, *iron foundry worker, Lancashire*

All things bright and beautiful,
All creatures great and small,
All things wise and wonderful,
The Lord God made them all.
He gave us eyes to see them,
And lips that we might tell
How great is God Almighty,
Who has made all things well.

Mrs C. F. Alexander (1818–95)

MARK TULLY, *broadcaster and correspondent from India*

Cast thy bread upon the waters: for thou shalt find it after many days. Give a portion to seven, and also to eight; for thou knowest not what evil shall be upon the earth.

If the clouds be full of rain, they empty themselves upon the earth: and if the tree fall toward the south, or toward the north, in the place where the tree falleth, there it shall be.

He that observeth the wind shall not sow; and he that regardeth the clouds shall not reap.

In the morning sow thy seed, and in the evening withhold not thine hand: for thou knowest not whether shall prosper, either this or that, or whether they both shall be alike good.

Ecclesiastes 11, verses 1–4 and 6 (Authorized Version)

JILLY COOPER, *author*

Prayer for an adopted child

Not flesh of my flesh
nor bone of my bone
but still, miraculous,
my own.
Never forget
for a single minute,
you didn't grow under my heart
but in it.

Anon.

'The adoption poem is a beautiful poem. It is anonymous and nobody seems to know who wrote it. I think it is a prayer although it is a poem, because it is so beautiful.'

DUDLEY DOUST, *author and sports writer*

From Pied Beauty

Glory be to God for dappled things –
For skies of couple-colour as a brinded cow;
For rose-moles all in stipple upon trout that swim;
Fresh-firecoal chestnut-falls; finches' wings;
Landscape plotted and pieced – fold, fallow, and plough;
And, all trades, their gear and tackle and trim.

Gerard Manley Hopkins (1844–1889)

'You need not be religious to be captured by the spiritual joy and
poetic fun expressed by Hopkins.'

Though I am different from you,
We were born involved
In one another.

Tao Ch'ien

PADDY HEAZELL, *retired prep school headmaster*

Green Blackboards

The school is up to date.
Proudly the principal tells of all the improvements.
The finest discovery, Lord, is the green blackboard.
The scientists have studied long, they have made
    experiments:
We know now that green is the ideal colour, that it
doesn't tire the eyes, that it is quieting and relaxing.

It has occurred to me, Lord, that you didn't wait so long
to paint the trees and meadows green.
    Your research laboratories were efficient, and in order
not to tire us, you perfected a number of shades of green
for your modern meadows.
    And so the 'finds' of men consist in discovering what
you have known from time immemorial.

    Thank you, Lord, for being the good Father who gives
his children the joy of discovering by themselves the
treasures of his intelligence and love,
    But keep us from believing that – by ourselves – we
have invented anything at all.

    Michel Quoist, translated by A. M. de Commaile and A. M. Forsyth

DEBORAH JONES, *former Editor of the* Catholic Herald

St Basil's Prayer for Animals

O God, enlarge within us a sense of fellowship with all living things, our brothers and sisters the animals, to whom you gave the earth as their home in common with us.

We remember with shame that in the past we have exercised the high dominion of man with ruthless cruelty, so that the voice of the earth, which should have gone up to you in song, has been a groan of travail.

May we realize that they live not for us alone but for themselves and for you, and that they love the sweetness of life.

St Basil (330–79)

TIM KIRKBRIDE, *retired company director*

From A Cowboy's Prayer

O Lord, I've never run where churches grow,
I've always loved Creation better as it stood
That day you finished it, so long ago,
And looked upon your work, and found it good.

Let me be easy on the man that's down
And make me square and generous with all;
I'm careless sometimes, Lord, when I'm in town,
But never let them call me mean or small.

'This prayer, in his own handwriting, was found among the books
of the late Elliot Perkins, who trained as a cowboy in his youth,
and later became Professor of History at Harvard University.

DR JONATHAN SACKS, *Chief Rabbi*

O my God, the soul which You placed within me is pure.
You created it, You formed it, You breathed it into me,
   and You preserve it within me.
You will one day take it from me, but will restore it to
   me in the hereafter.
So long as the soul is within me, I will give thanks to
   You, O Lord my God and God of my fathers, Master of
   all works, Lord of all souls. Blessed are You – the Lord,
   who restores the souls to the dead.

Ancient Jewish Traditional

'This prayer, taken from the daily morning service of the Jewish
prayer book, affirms the essential goodness of humanity, the gift of
life itself, and our need to be mindful that it is given to us by G–d
in order to do good while we are here on earth.'

THE RT. REVD DAVID SHEPPARD, *former Bishop of Liverpool*

Almighty God,
You have provided the resources of the world
To maintain the life of your children,
And have so ordered our life
That we are dependent upon each other.

Bless all people in their daily work,
And, as you have given us the knowledge to produce plenty,
So give us the will to bring it within reach of all;
Through Jesus Christ Our Lord. Amen.

Collect for Rogation Days, Alternative Service Book 1980

ROSEMARY SMYTH, *miller's wife*

From the prison of anxious thought that greed has builded,
From the fetters that envy has wrought, and pride has gilded,
From the noise of the crowded ways and the fierce confusion,
From the folly that wastes its days in a world of illusion,
(Ah, but the life is lost that frets and languishes there!)
I would escape and be free in the joy of the open air.

By the faith that the flowers show when they bloom unbidden,
By the calm of the river's flow to a goal that is hidden,
By the trust of the tree that clings to its deep foundation,
By the courage of wild birds' wings on the long migration,
(Wonderful secret of peace that abides in Nature's breast!)
Teach me how to confide, and live my life, and rest.

H. van Dyke (1852–1933)

Peace

THE RT. HON. TONY BLAIR, *Prime Minister*

A Psalm of the Sons of Korah

God is our refuge and strength,
A very present help in trouble.

Therefore we will not fear,
Even though the earth be removed,
And though the mountains be carried into the
midst of the sea;

Though its waters roar and be troubled,
Though the mountains shake with its swelling.

He makes wars cease to the end of the earth;
He breaks the bow and cuts the spear in two;
He burns the chariot in the fire.

Be still, and know that I am God.

Psalm 46, verses 1, 2, 3, 9 and 10
(New King James Version of the Bible)

RUTH GLEDHILL, *Religion Correspondent*, The Times

Lord, make me an instrument of your peace.
Where there is hatred let me sow love,
Where there is injury, pardon;
Where there is doubt, faith;
Where there is despair, hope;
Where there is darkness, light;
Where there is sadness, joy.
O divine Master, grant that I may not so much seek
To be consoled, as to console,
To be understood, as to understand,
To be loved, as to love;
For it is in giving that we receive;
It is in pardoning that we are pardoned;
It is in dying that we are born to eternal life. Amen.

Attributed to St Francis of Assisi,
this prayer first appeared in print in the 1920s

'I use this prayer every morning and night or even in the car or
Tube, also when frustrated by a provocative caller, a piece of mean-
ingless liturgy or a failure to succeed. It controls my quick temper
and puts life in perspective.'

LAMBETH DAY CENTRE FOR THE HOMELESS

You continue to call us to work for peace.
Our world is broken and wounded by injustice, violence and
    indifference.
Alone, we would be overwhelmed by the challenges that
    face us.
But together, supported by your Spirit,
we can do more than any one of us could dream or imagine.

Written for the fiftieth anniversary of the Pax Christi International
Movement in 1995

NORTHERN IRELAND SCHOOLCHILDREN

Peace in the city,
Peace in the house,
Peace in my heart,
And peace everywhere.

From 'A Prayer for Peace' by Joy Calvert,
Londonderry Primary School, and Alicia O'Rourke, St Finian's Primary

THE RT. HON. CHRISTOPHER PATTEN,
last Governor of Hong Kong

A Meditation

God has created me to do Him some definite service; He has committed some work to me which He has not committed to another. I have my mission – I may never know it in this life, but I shall be told it in the next.

I am a link in a chain, a bond of connection between persons. He has not created me for naught. I shall do good, I shall do His work. I shall be an angel of peace, a preacher of truth in my own place while not intending it – if I do but keep His Commandments.

Therefore, I will trust Him. Whatever, wherever I am, I can never be thrown away. If I am in sickness, my sickness may serve Him; in perplexity, my perplexity may serve Him; if I am in sorrow, my sorrow may serve Him. He does nothing in vain. He knows what He is about. He may take away my friends, He may throw me among strangers, He may make me feel desolate, make my spirits sink, hide my future from me – still He knows what He is about.

John Henry Newman (1801–90)

THE VERY REVD JOHN F. PETTY, *former Provost of Coventry*

Death of a Child

Eternal God, from whom every family in heaven and
   earth takes its name,
we remember today our child whom you lent us to love
   and is now taken from us.
Hold each one in peace today and forever,
and as we offer you our memories of their unfinished lives,
bring us at last to rejoice together in that light and
   love that have no end;
through your own Child who died and was raised to glory,
our Saviour Jesus Christ. Amen.

Michael Sadgrove, Provost of Sheffield

A Coventry Prayer

Almighty God, Father of us all,
you call us to make peace and to love and serve our
   neighbour.
May our City (and Cathedral) ruined and rebuilt,
be a sign to all peoples of the healing of old wounds.
Help us to build a kinder, more just world
where those of many races may live together in peace,
and all the human family be one;
through Jesus Christ our Lord. Amen.

Michael Sadgrove, Provost of Sheffield

THE REVD TREVOR WILLIAMS,
*Leader of the Corrymeela Community, an ecumenical community
of reconciliation in Northern Ireland*

Give us, Lord God, a vision of our world as your love
  would make it:
a world where the weak are protected, and none go
  hungry or poor;
a world where the benefits of civilized life are shared,
  and everyone can enjoy them;
a world where different races, nations and cultures
  live in tolerance and mutual respect;
a world where peace is built with justice, and justice
  is guided by love;
And give us the inspiration and courage to build it,
  through Jesus Christ our Lord. Amen.

Trevor Williams

'There are no quick fixes in the work of Reconciliation, it is a web
of "right relationships". One break destroys the whole. To work for
peace you need a clear vision to maintain your energy and nourish
your hope. The love of God alone brings this about.'

SYDNEY WOODERSON,
Olympic runner, mile and half-mile world record holder, 1937

O God, from whom all holy desires, all good counsels, and all just works do proceed; Give unto thy servants that peace which the world cannot give; that both our hearts may be set to obey thy commandments, and also that by thee we being defended from the fear of our enemies may pass our time in rest and quietness; through the merits of Jesus Christ our Saviour. Amen.

The Second Collect at Evening Prayer, Book of Common Prayer

KEN POOLE, *newspaper deliverer*

Dear Lord, once again we ask your help with this our prayer for peace. Grant us to seek the ways of talking and meeting instead of the ways of guns and war and that whatever our colour or creed we may be as one.

Ken Poole

Praise

VALERIE ELIOT, *widow of T. S. Eliot*

O Light Invisible, we praise Thee!
Too bright for mortal vision.
O Greater Light, we praise Thee for the less;
The eastern light our spires touch at morning,
The light that slants upon our western doors at evening,
The twilight over stagnant pools at batflight,
Moon light and star light, owl and moth light,
Glow-worm glowlight on a grassblade.
O Light Invisible, we worship Thee!

We thank Thee for the lights that we have kindled,
The light of altar and of sanctuary;
Small lights of those who meditate at midnight
And lights directed through the coloured panes of windows
And light reflected from the polished stone,
The gilded carven wood, the coloured fresco.
Our gaze is submarine, our eyes look upward
And see the light that fractures through unquiet water.
We see the light but see not whence it comes.
O Light Invisible, we glorify Thee!

From 'The Rock' by T. S. Eliot (1888–1965)

SIR JEREMY MORSE, *banker*

Blessed Lord, who hast caused all holy Scriptures to be written for our learning: Grant that we may in such wise hear them, read, mark, learn, and inwardly digest them, that by patience and comfort of thy holy Word, we may embrace, and ever hold fast the blessed hope of everlasting life, which thou hast given us in our Saviour Jesus Christ. Amen.

Collect for the second Sunday in Advent, Book of Common Prayer

THE RT. HON. THE COUNTESS MOUNTBATTEN OF BURMA

Lord, grant that I may catch a fish
So large that even I,
In speaking of it afterwards,
May have no need to lie!

Source unknown

OLIVE NEUMANN, *housewife*

Teach me, my God and King,
In all things Thee to see;
And what I do in anything,
To do it as for Thee.

From 'The Elixir' by George Herbert (1593–1633)

JENNIE THOMAS, *art teacher*

May the glory of the Lord endure for ever;
may the Lord rejoice in his works.

He looks at the earth, and it trembles;
he touches the mountains, and they smoke.

I will sing to the Lord all my life;
I will sing praise to my God as long as I live.

May my meditation be pleasing to him,
as I rejoice in the Lord.

Psalm 104, verses 31–34 (New International Version of the Bible)

ROSEMARY VEREY, *gardener and author*

O God, who hast prepared for them that love thee such
good things as pass man's understanding; Pour into our
hearts such love toward thee, that we, loving thee above
all things, may obtain thy promises, which exceed all
that we can desire; through Jesus Christ our Lord.
Amen.

Collect for the sixth Sunday after Trinity, Book of Common Prayer

TRUST

DAME CICELY SAUNDERS,
*President of St Christopher's Hospice, founder of
the hospice movement*

My lord god, I have no idea where I am going. I do not
see the road ahead of me. I cannot know for certain
where it will end. Nor do I really know myself, and the
fact that I think that I am following your will does not
mean that I am actually doing so. But I believe that the
desire to please you does in fact please you. And I hope
I have that desire in all that I am doing. I hope that I will
never do anything apart from that desire. And I know
that if I do this you will lead me by the right road though
I may know nothing about it. Therefore I will trust you
always though I may seem to be lost and in the shadow
of death. I will not fear, for you are ever with me, and
you will never leave me to face my perils alone.

*Thomas Merton (1915–68), a mystic and a Trappist monk of the Abbey
of Gethsemani, Kentucky*

DAME BARBARA SHENFIELD, *former Chairman of the WRVS*

O Lord,
'How small, of all that human hearts endure,
That part which laws or kings can cause
or cure!'
I put my trust in Thee.

From The Traveller *by Oliver Goldsmith (1728–74)*

SIR JOHN WILLS, *former Lord Lieutenant of Somerset*

O God, who knowest us to be set in the midst of so many and great dangers, that by reason of the frailty of our nature we cannot always stand upright; Grant to us such strength and protection, as may support us in all dangers, and carry us through all temptations; through Jesus Christ our Lord. Amen.

Collect for the fourth Sunday after Epiphany, Book of Common Prayer

'This prayer speaks to those who seek strength to meet personal challenges with a steadfast heart.'

THE RT. HON. LORD JUSTICE SCHIEMANN,
Lord Justice of Appeal

The Study of Law

Almighty God, Giver of Wisdom, without Whose help resolutions are vain, without Whose blessing study is ineffectual, enable me, if it be Thy will, to attain such knowledge as may qualify me to direct the doubtful, and instruct the ignorant, to prevent wrongs, and terminate contentions; and grant that I may use that knowledge, which I shall attain, to Thy glory and my own salvation, for Jesus Christ's sake.

Doctor Samuel Johnson (1709–84)

O Lord, my Maker and Protector, Who has graciously sent me into this world, to work out my salvation, enable me to drive from me all such unquiet and perplexing thoughts as may mislead or hinder me in the practice of those duties which Thou hast required. When I behold the works of Thy hands and consider the course of Thy providence, give me Grace always to remember that Thy thoughts are not my thoughts, nor Thy ways my ways. And while it shall please Thee to continue me in this world where much is to be done and little to be known, teach me by Thy Holy Spirit to withdraw my mind from unprofitable and dangerous enquiries, from difficulties vainly curious, and doubts impossible to be solved. Let me rejoice in the light which Thou hast imparted, let me serve Thee with active zeal, and humble confidence, and wait with patient expectation for the time in which the soul which Thou receivest, shall be satisfied with knowledge. Grant this, O Lord, for Jesus Christ's sake.

Doctor Samuel Johnson (1709–84)

JOSEPHINE SAWNEY, *organist*

Of what avail this restless, hurrying activity?
This heavy weight of earthly duties?
God's purposes stand firm,
And thou, His little one,
Needest one thing alone,
Trust in His power and He will meet thy need,
Thy burden resteth safe on Him;
And thou, His little one,
Mayest play securely at His side.
This is the sum and substance of it all.
God is,
God loveth thee,
God beareth all thy care.

Tukaram (1608–49), Indian peasant and mystic

Acknowledgements

Every effort has been made to locate copyright holders, although in a small number of cases this has proved impossible. We are grateful for permission to reprint the following copyright material. We also thank individuals who sent their own prayers.

Extracts from the Authorized Version of the Bible (The King James Bible), the rights in which are vested in the Crown, are reproduced by permission of the Crown's Patentee, Cambridge University Press.

Extracts from The Book of Common Prayer, the rights in which are vested in the Crown, are reproduced by permission of the Crown's Patentee, Cambridge University Press.

Scripture quotations from the New King James Version are reproduced by permission of Thomas Nelson, © 1979, 1980, 1982.

Scripture quotations from the Holy Bible New International Version, © 1973, 1978, 1984 by International Bible Society, are reproduced by permission of Hodder & Stoughton.

Scripture quotations from the Jerusalem Bible © 1966, 1967, 1968 are reproduced by permission of Darton Longman and Todd, and Doubleday.

Scripture quotations from the Amplified Bible are reproduced by permission of the Lockman Foundation.

Prayer from the Alternative Service Book 1980 is copyright © The Central Board of Finance of the Church of England and is reproduced with permission.

Kahlil Gibran: The National Committee of Gibran, for words from *The Prophet* (1951)

Andre Zirnheld: Little, Brown, for 'I Bring This Prayer to You, Lord', from *David Stirling: A Biography*, by Alan Hoe;

also Professor Alan Steele for the translation, and the L'Amicale des Anciens Parachutistes SAS et des Anciens Commandos de la France libre

Dag Hammarskjöld: Faber and Faber, for three prayers from *Markings*, translated by W. H. Auden

Dietrich Bonhoeffer: SCM Press Ltd, for 'O God, early in the morning', from *Morning Prayers* (1971)

T. S. Eliot: Faber and Faber, for lines of Choruses from 'The Rock X', from *Collected Poems 1909–1962*

Michel Quoist: Gill & Macmillan, for 'Green Blackboards', from *Prayers of Life*

David Adam: SPCK, for 'Come Holy Dove', from *Border Lands*

William Gaither: Kingsway's Thankyou Music for 'Because He Lives' © 1971

A. E. Housman: The Society of Authors, for 'Easter Hymn'

Michael Sadgrove: 'Death of a Child' and 'A Coventry Prayer'

Thomas Merton: Search Press and Burns & Oates, for 'My Lord God, I have no idea where I am going'

Peter Baelz: 'Generous God, Creator Spirit', by permission of the author

R. R. Broackes (compiler): SPCK, for 'Take Me This Day and Use Me', from *Unto the Hills* (1958)

Giles Harcourt (compiler): HarperCollins, for 'I Believe in the Sun', from *Short Prayers for the Long Day*

Matthew Tobias: The Welsh Guards, for their regimental collect